I Am a Book

by Linda Hayward

Illustrations by Carol Nicklaus

M Millbrook Press   Minneapolis

For Mallarie, Travis, Mahealani, Dylan, and Nikolai

Copyright © 2006 by Linda Hayward
Illustrations copyright © 2006 by Carol Nicklaus

Reading Consultant: Lea M. McGee, Ed.D.
Silly Millies and the Silly Millies logo are trademarks of Lerner Publishing Group.

Millbrook Press
A division of Lerner Publishing Group
241 First Avenue North
Minneapolis, MN 55401 U.S.A.
Website address: www.lernerbooks.com

Library of Congress Cataloging-in-Publication Data
Hayward, Linda.
I am a book / Linda Hayward ; illustrations by Carol Nicklaus.
p. cm.—(Silly Millies)
Summary: Describes how a book is created, manufactured, and distributed.
ISBN-13: 978-0-7613-2905-3 (lib. bdg.)
ISBN-10: 0-7613-2905-6 (lib. bdg.)
1. Books—Juvenile literature.   2. Book industries and trade—Juvenile literature.
3. Printing-—Juvenile literature.   [1. Books.   2. Book industries
and trade.   3. Printing.]   I. Nicklaus, Carol, ill.   II. Title.   III. Series.
Z116.A2 H38 2006   002—dc21   2002014846

Manufactured in the United States of America
1 2 3 4 5 6 — DP — 11 10 09 08 07 06

I Am
a Book

I am a book. I was
made to be read.
But here I am,
stuck on a shelf with
a bunch of other books.

How is anyone going to find me?

I want to have my pages turned.

I want to be read from cover to cover.

I am easy to get to know.
Just look at the picture
on my front cover.
It shows that there is
a funny story inside.
I am made of lots of pages.

I Am
a Book

I Am
a Book

by Linda Hayward
rated by Carol Nicklaus

I have two covers—

one in front and one in back.

They keep my pages nice and snug.

Go ahead, shake me.

Nothing will fall out.

I have a spine that holds me together.

The words and pictures on my pages
are my most important parts.
Who wrote them? Who drew them?
Who decided to make me
in the first place?
My title page has the answers.

Title Page

silly Millies

I Am a Book

by Linda Hayward
Illustrated by Carol Nicklaus

Millbrook Press Minneapolis

When was I made?

Just look at my copyright page to find out.

Copyright
Page

How many pages do I have in all?

Just look at the number on the last page.

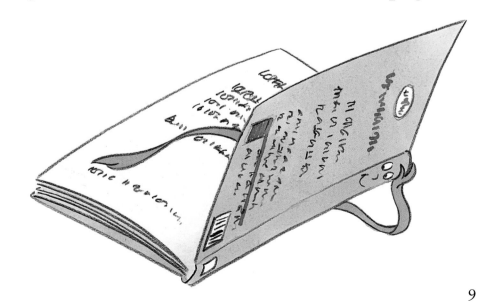

I was not always this interesting.
Before I was a book, I was just
a bunch of wood chips.
So how did I get to be a book
and not a campfire?
I went to the paper mill.

Most paper is made of fibers
that grow inside wood.
At the paper mill I go in
as a bunch of wood chips,
and I come out as fine paper.
I am on a roll.
Then I am off to
the printing company.

Here
I go!

The printer puts me in
a room full of other rolls.
I wait for the right story
to come along.
The right story is one that
will look great printed on me.

While I am waiting, I have
a wonderful daydream.
In my dream an author writes
a story about me.
It has a lot of words.

Other people come into my dream.
An editor checks all my
words—every single one!

An artist draws pictures
to go with the story.
She makes me look cute and funny!

A designer fits the words
and pictures together.
She invents my pages!

Now this is the best part.
The words and pictures
are printed—on me!

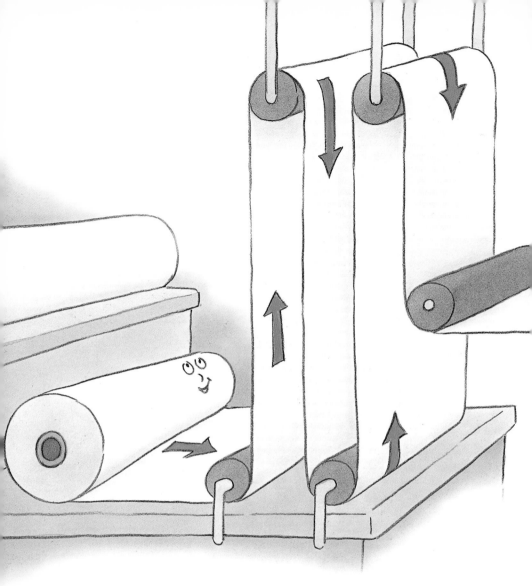

Suddenly I wake up.

My roll is loaded on the printing press.

I am moving fast.

A loud noise is all around me.

I feel as if I am inside a train engine.

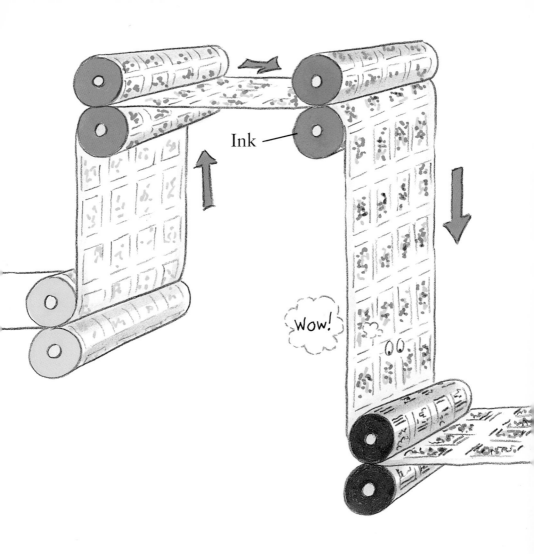

Ink

WoW!

I can smell wet ink.
Something is pressing the ink on me.
The ink is yellow, then red,
then blue, then black.

Soon I am covered
with words and pictures.
Hey! The pictures are
the pictures in my dream.

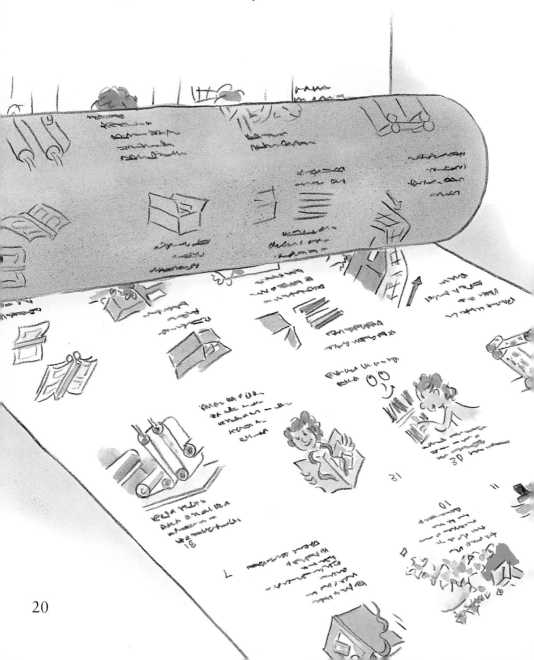

Dryer

The dryer dries my ink.
See how cute I am!
A trip through the printing press
changes you forever.

Next a blade cuts my roll
into sheets of paper.
Here I am—one big sheet,
printed on both sides!

Cutter

Folder

The folder folds my sheets.

Wow! All my pages are in order.

How did the machine do that?

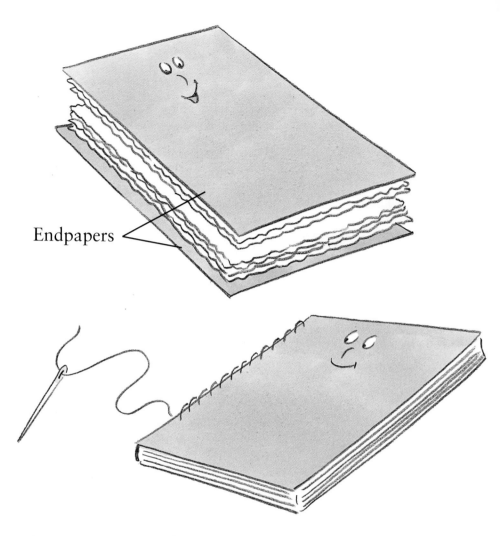

Endpapers

Next I go to the binding machine.

The binder lays me between two papers.

They are called endpapers.

Then we are all sewn together

to make me strong.

My sides are trimmed.

I am wrapped in a case. My covers
are glued onto the case, and
the case is glued to my endpapers.
I am pressed tight.

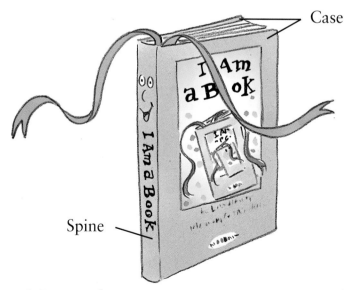

Case

Spine

Now I have a spine. I can stand up.
I am bound to be read now.

The printer puts me in a carton
with other books.
They look just like me.

A truck takes me to the publisher.

The publisher puts me in a box
with a bunch of different books.

A truck takes me to the library.
A library is a good home for a book.
I am glad I am not a gum wrapper!

I am given a library name.

It is EASY READER HAYWARD.

I am called EASY READER because

I am easy to read.

HAYWARD is my author's last name.

I ride to my row
on a cart.

That is how I came to be
stuck on this shelf.

Hey! Someone is coming down my row.
Someone is looking for my library name.
"E . . . F . . . G . . . H . . .
HAYWARD . . . Here it is!"
Someone has found me!

My pages are being turned.
Someone is laughing.
I know now that I am going
to be read from cover to cover.
I can hardly wait!

About the Author

Linda Hayward is the author of more than 60 easy-to-read books, including *A Day in the Life of a Firefighter, Little By Little*, and the companion volume to this book, *I Am a Pencil*, published by Millbrook in 2003. She has been writing children's books for 35 years. She lives in Naples, Florida, with her husband. The little book that narrates this tale has also been seen around her house on occasion.

Tips for Discussion

- Take a look at this book. How many parts can you name? Start with the physical parts of the book, then open it up and see how many printed parts you can name.

- Discuss the importance of books. What can you gain from reading books?

- Can you remember the steps in making a book? What has to happen first? What is the last step?